MW00785026

MOONSHINE, MUSIC
AND GHOSTS

Tony Brooks

Copyright © 2024 by Tony Brooks

ALL RIGHTS RESERVED.

No part of this book may be reproduced or transmitted in any form by any means, electronic or mechanical, including photocopying and recording, or by any information storage and retrieval system, except as may be expressly permitted in writing from the author.

ISBN: 978-1-965146-36-1

TABLE OF CONTENTS

PRE WORD

As a child, I was captivated by Mark Twain's "The Adventures of Tom Sawyer." Tom's escapades left a lasting impression on me, and throughout my life, I found myself drifting from one adventure to the next. In this book, I've shared many of those experiences about me, my family, and friends. I tried to relate the stories to the best of my memory for each episode. I hope you find as much enjoyment in reading about them as I did—most of the time—in living them.

CHAPTER 1
KICKED OUT!

When I was younger, I had the incredible opportunity to travel extensively, exploring over 20 different countries. Among these adventures, one of the most memorable was my journey to Egypt. My first visit to this ancient land was nothing short of extraordinary. I marveled at the Great Pyramid, wandered through the Valley of the Kings, and even experienced a camel ride—though that last one turned out to be more of an adventure than I had anticipated.

My first camel ride is a story I'll never forget. Unfamiliar with the ways of camels, I assumed they would rise like horses, lifting their front legs first. So, I braced myself accordingly. To my surprise, when the camel abruptly stood up on its hind legs, I was thrown forward, sailing over the camel's head. The air was filled with laughter, and while my pride took a hit, thankfully, I escaped without any physical injury.

The Great Pyramid, however, was the true highlight of my trip. Standing before this ancient wonder, I was awestruck by its grandeur. I spent a lot of time exploring its interior, descending into its depths, wandering through its mysterious chambers, and imagining what life might have been like during the height of the Egyptian Empire. The sense of history was palpable, and it was an experience that left a lasting impression on me.

I also enjoyed a trip to the Red Sea. This unique body of water is the lowest elevation on land and has an extremely high concentration of mineral salts. It is a good idea not to go swimming, more like floating, as you can't sink, with any cuts or abrasions as they will burn like crazy and you will not enjoy yourself very much. I spent a large chunk of my day just laying around and enjoying the site. I found out the next day after I had returned from the site, A terrorist attack took place at the site and several tourists were killed and several were wounded which just further shows how fortunate I was how the conflict in Israel was escalating.

One experience that has always stayed with me is my first arrival in Egypt. Before heading there, I was in London, tasked with a sensitive situation involving the American Embassy. A father had tragically passed away from a heart attack, leaving his two young sons alone in a foreign country. The boys were devastated, grappling with the loss of their father and the fear of being stranded in an unfamiliar land. My job was to ensure their safe return to the United States. Thankfully, I was able to arrange everything swiftly, securing their journey home with an embassy official accompanying them.

By the time I finished in London and caught my flight to Cairo, it was quite late. I arrived at my hotel around 9 p.m., exhausted from the day's events. My colleagues, knowing I was delayed, had kindly arranged a special dinner for me. There was a particular dish prepared that caught my eye. It looked delightful—a large pastry, resembling a fried apple pie or so I thought. Having been tied up all day and missing out on any meals, I was ravenous. Without hesitation, I helped myself to three of these tempting treats.

But as soon as I cut into the first one, an overwhelming smell hit me, almost causing me to lose my composure right there at the table. Not wanting to insult my hosts, and unsure if the pastries had simply gone bad from sitting out, I somehow managed to choke down all three. As soon as I politely excused myself, I rushed to the nearest restroom and promptly emptied my stomach. From that day forward, I vowed to always inquire about the food I was offered in advance. I could have declined that dish, but my hunger—and my love for sweets—got the better of me.

My second trip to Egypt, however, did not unfold as smoothly or end as well as the first. The journey began pleasantly enough, with visits to several countries before I headed to Cairo. Upon landing, everything seemed fine until I reached customs. As soon as I presented my passport, the agents summoned two soldiers and had me detained.

I was completely taken aback by this turn of events. Confusion and a fair amount of fear set in as I had no idea what was happening. I was led to a small room inside the airport, with a single entrance and exit, and seated at a desk. A guard was stationed inside the room, while another, armed with a military rifle, stood outside. I attempted to engage the soldiers in conversation, but they remained silent.

Hours passed, with no explanation from either airport or military personnel. Despite my repeated requests to contact the American Embassy, I was met with silence. Eventually, an Egyptian military officer and a civilian official entered the room and began interrogating me about my reasons for being in Cairo and the country I had arrived from. None of it made sense to me. Then, out of nowhere, they accused me of being an Israeli spy.

That accusation instantly grabbed my attention and filled me with dread. I was aware that Israel and Egypt were at war, but until that moment, I hadn't given it much thought. Now, the gravity of the situation hit me, and I became genuinely frightened.

The questioning continued for hours as I repeatedly denied any connection to Israel, Mossad, or any Israeli agency. I insisted I was of Irish descent and a U.S. citizen, demanding my right to speak with the American Embassy. They left for about an hour and then returned, resuming the same line of questioning, still convinced I was a spy.

Finally, after what felt like an eternity, I was informed that they didn't believe me and that I was no longer welcome in Egypt. I was to be escorted out of the airport and taken to a different airfield, where I would be placed on a military plane bound for a neutral country—Lebanon. In short, I was being kicked out of Cairo, Egypt.

I was loaded onto a twin-engine aircraft, with two guards seated on the floor near the wing on the right side, keeping a close eye on me. The flight itself was a nightmare. From my seat, I could see the wing flapping up and down like a bird's wing, and the noise and turbulence were intense. I was convinced the plane was going to crash.

Never in my life have I been so relieved as when I finally landed at the airport in Lebanon. The sight of military personnel patrolling the area and machine gun emplacements didn't exactly put me at ease, but at least I was out of Egypt. After being escorted into the airport, I was handed over to local authorities to continue my journey.

Later, I discovered the cause of my trouble in Egypt. The agency that arranged my flights was supposed to provide separate tickets—one showing my flight into Egypt and onward to Lebanon, and another, not to be shown in Egypt, for my flight to Tel Aviv, Israel. However, my ticket indicated a direct flight from Cairo to Tel Aviv, a route that was impossible given the ongoing war between Israel and Egypt. This misunderstanding led to my expulsion from Egypt.

And as for getting kicked out of Prague in the Czech Republic—that's a story for another day.

CHAPTER 2
THE SAME DONKEY....

While on the subject of travel, I once flew from Athens, Greece, to Israel, where I spent several days exploring some of the most spectacular sites the country has to offer, particularly in Jerusalem.

In Jerusalem, I visited the Western Wall, a sacred site for Jewish prayer and reflection. I also stood in awe at the Church of the Holy Sepulchre, revered as the site of Jesus' crucifixion and resurrection. Walking along the Via Dolorosa, the path believed to have been taken by Jesus on his way to the crucifixion, was a profoundly moving experience.

I enjoyed a few moments of quiet solitude in the Garden of Gethsemane, located on the Mount of Olives. This spot not only holds deep spiritual significance but also offers breathtaking views of the Old City. At night, the walls of the city are illuminated, creating a mesmerizing sight.

Beyond Jerusalem, I explored Nazareth, the city where Jesus is believed to have spent his youth. The Basilica of the Annunciation was a highlight of my visit there. Another unforgettable stop was the Sea of Galilee, a serene freshwater lake surrounded by historic sites such as Capernaum and the Mount of Beatitudes.

I also visited Caesarea, an ancient Roman city with impressive ruins, including a grand amphitheater and an aqueduct. While taking in the spectacular views one day, I felt my foot being gently lifted. Looking down, I saw a young boy, no older than 8 or 9, busily shining my shoe with a small shoeshine kit. His focus and determination made me laugh, and I rewarded him with a generous tip.

Now let me share a funny story that happened to me in Jerusalem, Israel.

I've been fortunate enough to travel to over 20 different countries, and Israel was one of them. I visited Israel on two separate occasions and thoroughly enjoyed exploring all the places mentioned in the Bible. It felt like the Bible came to life before my eyes every day I was there. I could almost see Jesus, his disciples, the people of Jerusalem, and the Romans acting out their roles in history. If you've never been, you should definitely go.

One morning, I decided to visit the Mount of Ascension, where it is believed that Jesus ascended into heaven. There's a stone slab there with a footprint that many believe is from Jesus himself. The day was overcast, and I'd heard there might be some light showers, but I decided to go anyway. The pathway to the Mount of Ascension was a broad, long walkway with a gentle incline, as best I can remember—it was quite a few years ago.

As I made my way up the path, I was about halfway when I was stopped by a Jewish gentleman dressed in what seemed to be traditional attire, reminiscent of the days of Jesus. He had a small donkey with him and offered to let me ride it to the top for a fee. We went back and forth about it, as I really didn't want to ride the donkey. I'm a pretty big guy, and this was a very small donkey—it just didn't seem like a good match. After some debate, he came back with what is probably the best sales pitch I've ever heard. In broken English, he said, 'You ride my donkey. This the best donkey in the world. This the same donkey Jesus rode!'

Wow, what a sales line. Needless to say, I didn't ride the donkey. I walked up to the Mount of Ascension and spent some time there, but that wasn't the end of the story. As I started back down the path, it began to rain lightly—not a heavy shower, just a misty drizzle. As I approached the spot where I'd met the old Jewish gentleman, I saw that he had finally convinced a tourist to take him up on his offer. I stopped to watch, certain that I was about to witness one of the funniest scenes I'd seen in a long time. The issue was, the donkey was very small, and the woman who was about to ride weighed well over 300 pounds.

It didn't take long for the scene I expected to unfold. She tried to mount the donkey several times, with the Jewish gentleman's help, but without success. Finally, on the last attempt, she managed to get on, but the donkey's legs simply flattened out, and she went rolling off the donkey and down the hill in the misty rain. For all I know, she might still be rolling downhill somewhere.

I feel fortunate to have witnessed such moments in my life.

CHAPTER 3
KICKED OUT AGAIN....

Continuing on the theme of travel, I have a somewhat scary story from my visit to Prague, Czechoslovakia. I had flown in, eager to explore the city—visit the castle, walk the Charles Bridge, see the famous cathedral, and spend time in the town square. I was ready to dive into everything Prague had to offer. However, history had other plans. I checked into my hotel, looking forward to a good night's sleep and an early start to my day of exploration.

During the night, I woke up to the sound of heavy vehicles rumbling through the streets. When I looked out from my hotel room, I saw Soviet tanks, heavy trucks, and soldiers moving through the city. As you might imagine, this immediately caught my attention. There was no gunfire, just the sound of military vehicles and an eerie silence from the people of Prague. It was as if the Soviets had simply moved in and taken over.

I wasn't sure what to do, but that decision was made for me. The Soviets ordered all non-citizens staying in hotels, or at least in the hotel where I was, to leave Prague immediately. We were told to gather our belongings and report to a bus waiting downstairs. I hurriedly packed up, boarded the bus, and we were driven to the airport. The atmosphere was tense as we went through customs and were escorted to a gate for our departure.

Airports are usually bustling with noise—people talking, announcements blaring, the general hum of activity. But when we arrived at the gate, the silence was almost deafening. I swear, if I had dropped a pin that day, it would have echoed like a bell. Everyone was somber and quiet, just sitting and staring out the windows. Soviet officials came around, collecting everyone's cameras, and they didn't return them when we finally left.

As we waited, I watched a massive Soviet plane land and taxi to the gate next to ours. Soldiers rolled out a long, wide red carpet, flanked by more soldiers standing at attention. Important dignitaries disembarked, escorted by the military. The entire scene felt surreal.

Eventually, our group was loaded onto a waiting jet. The silence on board was eerie—no one spoke, not even the pilot. After what felt like an eternity, the plane taxied to the runway, and we prepared for takeoff. But just as we were about to leave the ground, the power seemed to cut out, and the plane abruptly stopped. I looked out the window and saw flashing lights everywhere. The plane turned back and entered a holding pattern in a secluded area away from the airport.

We sat in total silence for what must have been twenty minutes, with no word from the crew. Then, the door opened, and a group of soldiers boarded, accompanied by a man who looked straight out of a spy movie—long black coat belted at the waist, black brimmed hat, dark sunglasses. They slowly walked through the cabin, glaring at each passenger, before entering the cockpit and closing the curtain behind them.

We continued to wait in silence for another twenty to thirty minutes, still with no explanation. Finally, the soldiers and the mysterious man walked back through the cabin and exited the plane. The door closed, and about fifteen minutes later, the pilot taxied back to the runway. This time, we actually took off. A collective sigh of relief swept through the cabin. To this day, I don't know what that delay was all about, but I'm just glad we got out of there.

I decided then and there that I would never visit Prague again!

CHAPTER 4
BAMA MOONSHINE.....

I grew up in North Alabama, where my father, his dad, and his brothers were involved in the moonshine trade, covering several counties. Even today, many counties in the area remain dry, meaning alcohol cannot be legally purchased. As I got older, I began hearing stories about my dad during his moonshine days. Tales of my grandfather's stills, hidden all over the mountains of North Alabama, still circulate today.

One story that stands out involves my father making a moonshine run in his 1949 Ford, which he fondly called "Leap and Leaner." While navigating the winding mountain roads, a sheriff's patrol car spotted him and gave chase. As the story goes, during the heat of the pursuit, one of the tires went flat. My dad managed to slide to a stop at the top of a steep hill, quickly jumped out, opened the trunk, grabbed the spare tire and jack, and got to work. In a flurry of action, he jacked up the car, removed the lug nuts, swapped out the flat tire, lowered the car, and sped off down the hill—all before the sheriff could catch up. The way I heard it, my dad was like a super tire changer, outwitting the law with his speed and skill.

To give you a better understanding, it's important to know what was happening in those counties during that time, particularly in the county where my dad lived. My family had stills in the mountains, producing moonshine that was delivered to various counties. The moonshine was transported in cars with false tanks and sold pint by pint to people across different areas. The local sheriff seemed to have a vendetta against my dad and was always trying to catch him. There were numerous chases on those old, unpaved gravel roads, with the sheriff relentlessly pursuing my dad and his brothers.

Years later, I asked my dad about the story during one of my visits. I found it hard to believe that anyone could pull off such a feat. He laughed and said it didn't happen quite the way I'd heard. Then, he shared the real story.

He explained that while making a run in his '49 Ford, he had just reached the top of a hill when his left rear tire blew out, causing him to slide to a stop. He got out, checked the road behind him, and saw no one as far as he could see. He retrieved the jack and spare tire and began changing the flat. Just as he started removing the lug nuts, he noticed headlights starting up the mountain. He had a gut feeling that it was the sheriff's car and knew he had to move quickly. He removed the last lug nut, tossed the flat tire into the ditch, and hurriedly placed the spare tire on the rim. He tightened only two lug nuts, jumped into the car, and sped off, driving right off the jack and leaving it behind. Sure enough, it was the sheriff, who immediately turned on his flashing lights and gave chase. My dad managed to lose him on those twisting mountain roads and finished his run, later adding the rest of the lug nuts to the rear tire.

It sounds like something straight out of one of those old country moonshine movies, like *Thunder Road*.

CHAPTER 5
RUNNING FROM THE ABC'S.....

Another story I heard about my dad involved an encounter with federal ABC (Alcohol, Tobacco, and Firearms) agents. These were the men responsible for catching moonshiners and enforcing the laws of the day concerning tobacco products, drugs, firearms, and other criminal activities. Their job was to seek out locations where moonshiners hid their stills for manufacturing white lightning (illegal whiskey) and other illicit liquors and to arrest and prosecute men like my grandfather and his family—which I'm a part of, just saying.

In this particular instance, the story goes like this: My grandfather, my dad, my dad's brother, and several men who worked for my grandfather were taking a load of 100-pound bags of sugar out to one of their stills in the mountains. The terrain was too rough for vehicles, so they had to carry the sugar on their backs, making several trips. This was nothing new to them; they were used to the grueling work. So, they loaded the sugar onto their backs and started the trek into the still area.

At a typical still site, there were the men who worked the still and others who were responsible for securing the area. Later on, they discovered that one of their men had been turned by a federal agent and had revealed the location of this particular still, as well as the plans for the new 100-pound sugar loads.

The men began walking the sugar into the mountains, and once they were inside the perimeter of the still, the ABC agents sprang from their hiding spots in the trees and bushes, shouting, "Federal agents, everybody freeze!" My grandfather quickly yelled to his men, "Run! Everyone for themselves!" to counter the agents' command.

Chaos erupted as the moonshiners scattered, each with an agent chasing after them. As the story was told to me, my dad took off down a trail with an agent hot on his heels. My dad was thin, strong, and a fast runner, so he sprinted up and down the hollers, staying just ahead of the ABC man behind him. The chase went on for quite some time, taking them from the clearing where the still was located to another mountain—Alabama has a lot of mountains—with the stubborn agent still in pursuit.

My dad said he ran until he was about to drop from exhaustion, but then he realized something—the ABC man was no longer behind him. That's when he noticed that he still had the 100-pound sack of sugar on his shoulder. He dumped the sack, made his way back to his car, and got out of the area, returning to town.

As before, I told my dad I found it hard to believe that he outran a federal agent with a 100-pound sack of sugar on his shoulder. He laughed and said that, in this case, it was the truth. He explained that when the ABC agents jumped out, he was so scared that all he could think about was getting away. He didn't want to get caught, so he reacted instinctively and started running, not even realizing he still had the sugar on his shoulder until the agent was no longer behind him. That's when he finally dumped it.

The results from this ABC raid are they did not catch any of my grandfathers crew. My grandfather and his crew knew the mountains like the back of their hands and the ABC men did not.

Just that simple. His only loss was the sugar and the Still location, which was no longer usable,

Wow, another story where you have to judge for yourself. I still find it hard to believe, but in my dad's defense, I never knew him to lie about anything.

CHAPTER 6
LIKE FATHER LIKE SON....
SORT OF.....

I've shared a few tales about my father, the Alabama moonshiner. After he was caught by the Federals for running moonshine, he served some time in prison and was advised to leave Alabama. "You best leave the state," they told him, "before you find yourself in more trouble than you can handle." I suppose it runs in the family, getting kicked out of places! During this period, my dad moved to Chicago, IL, where I spent a lot of my formative years, though I still returned to Alabama for most summers.

At the time, I was a teenager in high school, and I would've been considered, rightly so, one of the bad boys. A group of us hung out together, regularly finding ourselves in trouble. I was a frequent visitor to the principal's office, always for one reason or another.

One day, after I got into a fight with a guy, the principal, sat me down in his office. "You've got a knack for trouble, don't you?" he said, leaning back in his chair.

"Wasn't my fault," I muttered, rubbing my bruised jaw. "He hit first."

"That may be, but you're the one suspended," the principal replied, handing me the slip. "You need to find a better way to spend your energy."

But I wasn't one to listen. I cut classes on a regular basis and even ran a little side business, providing fake notes from doctors or parents to get kids back into class after they cut. It worked like a charm for a long time.

Once, we concocted something we called skunk perfume. "This'll clear out the school for sure," one of the guys said, shaking the bottle with a wicked grin.

We ran from one end of the building to the other, across all four floors, tossing bottles of this foul-smelling mixture into classrooms. The stench was so bad it could make you want to throw up, and we ended up emptying the school for most of the day.

Even though I was a rowdy troublemaker, I actually had top grades. In grammar school, I got two double promotions, skipping a grade entirely. Smart but trouble—that was me for sure, at least back then.

After my dad was forced to move to Chicago, he kept up his moonshining business, just shifting operations to the Chicago area. He made regular trips to Alabama to meet with his brother and my grandfather, bringing back trailers loaded with pints and half-pints of white lightning. He rented a garage separate from our house to store his loads.

Being the sweet young bad boy I was, I knew where my dad kept his booze. I "confiscated" several pints and half-pints and took them to school. "What's in the bags?" one of the guys asked when we met up outside school.

"You'll see," I said, handing him one of the bags.

As we walked toward school, the school cop pulled up beside us. "Why aren't you boys in class?" he demanded, eyeing us suspiciously.

"We, uh, had a late start," I lied, trying to keep my voice steady.

"Put the bags down and spread," he ordered, and I carefully set mine on the ground, praying the bottles wouldn't clink.

After frisking us for weapons and finding nothing, he said, "Get to school. And don't let me catch you out here again."

We picked up our bags, hearts pounding and headed to our hideaway at the deli across from the school

That day went down in infamy at my high school. Just about every kid was walking around drinking a mix of white lightning and pop. "This stuff's strong!" someone yelled as they took a swig.

Several students were expelled for indecent exposure, fighting, cussing out teachers, and breaking windows. Somehow, the principal's car was flipped over, and the school cop's car ended up with all four tires flattened.

All thanks to white lightning, made in Alabama, USA.

There's justice in life—my dad found out. "You did what?" he roared, reaching for a tree branch.

That was one of the longest days of my life. He wore out that branch on my backside and grounded me for months. "You better have learned your lesson," he warned.

Believe me, I did. I didn't pull a stunt like that again.

CHAPTER 7

CAT IN A BAG

I spent a large portion of my younger years in north Alabama, where me, my buddies, and cousins were constantly getting into jams with our parents due to our wild escapades. I doubt teenagers in other parts of the country got into the same kinds of predicaments we did.

Like every other kid in America, we played cowboys and Indians, except we did it with BB guns. I can tell you from experience that BBs hurt like the dickens when you get shot with them. I constantly had welts on my body from being hit. Looking back, it's a miracle none of us lost an eye, our hearing, or worse, each time we imitated our TV heroes and villains.

Growing up in the South, we had our own way of doing things. We hunted and fished throughout the year, though I suspect men like to fish mostly because it's a good excuse to drink beer and drown worms. Alabama is known for its poisonous snakes—rattlesnakes, water moccasins, and copperheads are the big ones. My cousin, nicknamed Copperhead, and I (they called me Cotton Top because of my shock of white-blond hair) spent a lot of time catching snakes. We turned them in for the bounty, which bought us plenty of candy.

Back then, it was just something we did. I'd use a forked stick I carved into a "Y" shape to catch the snakes behind the head, then finish them off. My cousin was braver—he'd distract them with one hand and reach around with the other to grab them. I guess he had more guts than me.

Snake wrangling didn't stick with me for long, as an incident during my time working at a GM plant can attest. I was the dispatcher, responsible for controlling all material movements inside the buildings. My role included managing a team of forklift drivers, truck spotters, clerks, and switchyard crews. At some point, someone had the bright idea that I'd be more effective if I were stationed out on the warehouse floor, so they set up a mobile office for me. It was a tiny space that could be moved to different locations around the plant, with the help of one of my forklift drivers.

This mobile office was just big enough to squeeze in a desk and file cabinet, and I had to slide in sideways to sit at my desk—it was a really tight fit. One day, I was coordinating with one of my truck spotters, who was moving a large assembly from one plant to another. Everything was running smoothly until, suddenly, my door flew open, and someone threw what looked like a snake across my desk.

Before I even had time to think, I tore through that tiny office trying to escape. I was so panicked I knocked one of the door hinges loose, and the door ended up hanging crooked. It wasn't until I got outside that I realized the "snake" was fake. The culprit, one of my drivers, thought it was the funniest thing in the world. He laughed so hard I thought he'd pass out.

Well, I didn't find it so amusing. After that day, that driver found himself on every dirty job I could think of, including garbage duty, for a whole month. Eventually, he begged me to stop and apologized for the prank. Safe to say, after that, I wasn't quite the brave snake wrangler I used to be.

One summer, my buddies and I were perpetually broke. All we wanted to do was party, and work didn't quite fit into that plan. Eventually, we came up with a brilliant—though reckless—way to keep our car running on empty pockets. Farmers often kept gas pumps on their properties for filling up tractors, combines, and other equipment, and we figured they wouldn't miss a tank or two. So, late at night, we'd roll up to some farm, pull up to the pump, and quietly fill our car's gas tank. Back then, nobody bothered to lock up their pumps, and for a while, our scheme worked like a charm.

One night, we set out as usual, laughing and whispering as we approached the farm we'd hit a few times before. Everything was quiet; we thought we were in the clear. We parked, got out, and started pumping gas. But just as we were halfway through, the whole farmyard suddenly lit up—floodlights flashing on from every angle.

The farmhouse door burst open, and out came the farmer, shouting and charging toward us with a double-barrel shotgun in hand. Panic hit us like a punch to the gut. We dropped everything, bolted for the car, and scrambled to get it started. Just as we peeled out, the farmer fired both barrels. We heard the unmistakable ping of pellets hitting the back of the car as we sped down the dirt road, hearts pounding.

By the time we made it back to town, we'd made a pact. That was the last time we'd "borrow" gas from a farmer. We knew we'd barely escaped and weren't eager to test our luck a second time.

Our idea of a swimming pool was pushing cows out of the way so we could swim in cattle watering holes. We even skinny-dipped when no one was around. Farmers hated it, of course, since it spooked the cattle, but we didn't care. The worst part was accidentally getting a mouthful of that water—not a taste I recommend.

Being so familiar with the creatures that lived in the North Alabama mountains brings me to the story of this chapter. One of those creatures is the bobcat, or lynx—a medium-sized wild cat with a temper so nasty it could probably rule the world if it were lion-sized. A bobcat would give a Tasmanian devil nightmares.

My buddy's dad was a veterinarian, and he always had animals around his house, which doubled as his office. One time, he had a bobcat in a cage, and we hatched a plan to have some fun with it—and get even with the guys from the next town over. They had pulled some pranks on us (stories for another time), so we figured it was payback time.

We tranquilized the bobcat, which we named Bob, and stuffed him into a large suitcase. Then we drove over to the next town and left the suitcase by a stop sign, right before the drive-in diner where everyone went after football games. Bob was making small noises by this point, starting to wake up.

It didn't take long before a carload of guys pulled up and stopped at the sign. They sat there longer than usual, then drove off—and, sure enough, the suitcase was gone.

We watched as the car drove about five lengths away, then suddenly the brake lights came on, and all the doors flew open. Five guys shot out of that car like it was on fire. Sure enough, Bob came barreling out of the car, hissing, spitting, and growling like a demon. The guys ran as if the devil himself were after them.

We were doubled over in laughter. I'll never forget how fast they ran or the look on their faces.

Oh yeah, we got in trouble yet again with My buddy's father who said we were no longer allowed in his shop again. My buddy was grounded over losing Bob.

Almost as good as the gator in a trunk. But that's another story for another time.

Man, what a night.

CHAPTER 8
THE BEATINGS STOPPED…..

My dad was well-liked and respected in Alabama. Many folks called him "Jack" because he always carried a hawkbill knife in the pocket of his overalls (like a jack Knife) and could whip it out in a flash. He ran a grocery store, a taxi service, and a corner café with my grandmother, and, of course, he was a big-time moonshiner. Over the years, he loaned out a lot of money to people in our small town and county. A few years ago, I came across an old logbook that showed the names of those he had lent money to, and most of them never paid it back. I asked him about it, and he just shrugged, saying he was glad he was able to help those people when they needed it. That logbook showed hundreds of thousands of dollars still owed, but he eventually threw it away, knowing the debts would never be settled. So over all he was not a bad guy.

But I don't want to paint the wrong picture of my dad. He was a man you couldn't push around -------tough as nails. I remember one time when he confronted a good ol' boy who owed him money for whiskey he had taken on consignment. When Dad asked him about payment, the man said, "You know what, old man? You can't get blood out of a turnip." I barely saw my dad move, but in an instant, he had that man pinned against the wall, his hawkbill knife under his throat. "No, but I can get the turnip. Give me my money now," Dad growled. The man fumbled in his pockets and handed over a wad of cash. Dad wasn't someone you messed with.

He could be great to others, but at home, he was a different man. He was on the mean side, especially to his own family. He beat me and my older sister countless times with belts and switches. Sometimes we deserved it for the trouble we got into, but other times, it was just because he was angry about something or other. One night, my sister stayed out later than she was supposed to and tried to sneak into the house without our dad waking up. Instead of heading to her own room, which was all the way at the other end of the house, she slipped through the front door near my bedroom and lay across my bed, hoping she could avoid him there. She was certain he'd hear her and that she'd be in trouble—but she had no idea he was already awake and waiting.

I was fast asleep and had no clue she was there when my dad came into my room, belt in hand. Without warning, he brought it down hard, aiming at my sister but hitting me instead. I jumped up, shouting, "What did I do, Daddy? I didn't do anything! Why are you whipping me?" Only then did I realize it was my sister he was after.

She ended up getting it pretty bad that night, but I had a nice belt mark on my back, too.

I remember one time I had terrible pain in my tooth, so Dad finally took me to the dentist. I had a deathly fear of needles—after an injury required me to get a bunch of shots in a short time—and I fought the dentist as hard as I could. The dentist called in his assistants, even the other dentist, and my dad tried to hold me down, but I wouldn't let them get that needle in my mouth. Dad was furious. He took me home, locked me in the pantry, and beat the hell out of me while my mom and sister pounded on the door, screaming for him to stop. Afterward, he took me right back to the dentist, and I sat there, quiet as a mouse, while they worked on me. I didn't dare move.

He was extremely jealous, too. He constantly accused my mom of flirting with other men, which usually led to him beating her up. This was a regular occurrence during my childhood. He worked the night shift at the GM plant, and before he left for work, he would clean the bottoms of my mom's shoes. When he came home, he would check to see if they were dirty, demanding to know where she had been, and that would often spark another argument—and another beating.

We didn't fully understand how bad it was until we were older. My dad and I did not get along, so I moved out and went to live with my uncle on my mom's side. I started working as a tile mechanic, laying floor and wall tile in housing projects and new constructions like Kmart stores.

One evening, after I got home to my uncle's place, my sister called. She had slipped out of the house so she could call to tell me Dad had beaten Mom again, and this time, it was bad. Something snapped in me. I saw red. I jumped in my car and sped toward their house, which was about an hour and a half away. The fog was so thick that night you could barely see the car in front of you, but I didn't care. I was doing 80, 90 miles per hour on those back roads, passing cars blindly. I didn't care if I crashed. I was too angry to think straight.

When I finally got there, I didn't even stop. I slid the car right up into the yard, jumped out, and slammed the front door open just as Dad was walking in from the kitchen. He stopped and stared at me, surprised. I was beyond caring. I shouted, "This is the last time you will ever beat my mother. You're going to pack your things and leave this house, and you're never coming back. I came here today ready to die, or for you to die. I don't care which, but the beatings stop today!"

He stood there for a few moments, silent. I was sure he was going to pull his knife on me, but he didn't. Then, without a word, he turned, walked into their bedroom, packed a few things, and left the house. My mother and father were never together again after that night.

That was the day the beatings stopped.

After my parents divorced, my mother found a small bit of satisfaction in a situation that developed with my dad. She and her sister, my aunt, would go out to dinner and dance from time to time. Despite the divorce, my dad—still the jealous, possessive man he'd always been—couldn't help himself from following her around. I guess some habits die hard.

One evening, as my mom and aunt headed out to dinner, they noticed my dad's car parked discreetly about a block away from the restaurant. His attempts to keep tabs on her weren't new, but this time, something was different. As they went back to my mom's car, a strange noise came from the trunk, like a muffled thump or a shifting weight. It didn't take long for them to put the pieces together—my dad had crawled into her trunk, pressing it down from the inside to make it look closed, all in a desperate attempt to follow her without being noticed.

Rather than confront him, my mom decided to turn this absurd situation to her advantage. She walked up to the car, pretending to notice that the trunk wasn't fully latched. With a grin she could barely suppress, she and my aunt slammed the trunk shut, trapping him inside. Then, without a second thought, they got into her car and drove off. But they didn't just drive off—they took the longest, bumpiest route they could find, hitting every pothole and rut on the way. Finally, she parked at home, went inside, and went to bed, leaving him to figure his own way out.

Later, my mom found out that he'd had to break out of the trunk and walk for miles to find somewhere he could call for a ride. I can only imagine the frustration—and maybe a bit of self-reflection—he felt on that long, lonely walk.

That night might have been rough for my dad, but for my mom, it was a small, well-deserved victory—a little taste of justice for all those years of jealousy and control.

In a rare moment of honesty, my dad once admitted to my sister that he knew my mom had never cheated on him or done half the things he'd accused her of. He just couldn't help himself. My sister believed his obsession went back to his own childhood. Our grandfather had constantly cheated on my grandmother, dragging my dad along as a young boy when he went to see other women. Those early memories of infidelity and betrayal left a lasting mark on him, shaping the man he became.

In the end, maybe the real culprit wasn't my dad, but my grandfather, who'd handed down a legacy of distrust and insecurity.

CHAPTER 9

JUST ANOTHER WORKDAY...

I spent a lot of my formative years working for my uncles, who were in the floor and wall tile business. Even while I was still in school, I worked on numerous housing projects and large-scale buildings like Kmart and warehouse buildings. I had four uncles who were journeyman tile mechanics—among the best in the business. They made laying beautiful walls and floors look easy. From them, I learned a great deal about construction and remodeling, knowledge that I've applied to every house I've owned over the years. I even became a member of the carpenters union (tile mechanics fall under that union) and worked in it for many years.

On large projects like Kmart or Jewel stores, my uncles and I would often race each other to see who could lay tile the fastest. The loser had to buy beer for the evening. We'd race in several categories—spreading the emulsion adhesive across rows, laying full tiles, doing cold cuts (straight cuts), and hot cuts (curved, corners, and doorways). We worked hard and fast, and there were plenty of evenings spent drinking beer afterward. Back then, we were known as speed tile mechanics, not custom ones.

Over the years, several funny episodes have stood out.

One was during a typical day working on a housing project. We usually had a system: one person would go in first to clean and patch the floors, then move on to the next house. Another would come in, measure and lay out the floor plan, spread the emulsion, and then move on to the next house. My uncle and I would follow, laying full tiles throughout the house. Then we'd do the cold cuts, hot cuts, clean up, and install the cove base on the walls.

During these long days, I used to sing while I worked. Later, my brother and I formed a band that played throughout the Midwest for five-plus years, but that's another story. Back then, I'd be singing along to whatever was playing on the radio. My uncles would often request different songs, and I'd switch over without thinking much of it. It wasn't until years later that I realized why they were so specific about their requests. It turned out I worked faster when I sang faster-paced songs! So, naturally, they always requested the upbeat ones. Sneaky uncles...

Another memorable episode involved my uncle, who was the foreman of the company. He assigned me and my other uncle, to work on a housing project in a Chicago suburb. He also asked us to do a custom tile job on the side for him after hours, promising to pay us separately. The job was for the mayor of the suburb, and we were to lay cork-tone tiles in the basement, using four different variations of light and dark shades.

We agreed and set out to the housing project. Along the way, we picked up a couple of six-packs and drank them while working. At lunchtime, we grabbed some more beer for the afternoon. After we finished for the day, we headed over to the mayor's house, picking up a case of beer on the way. By the time we started working, it was getting dark, so we had to string up lights to see. We went through the process: cleaning up, patching, laying the tiles, doing the cold and hot cuts, and finishing the cove base. By 1 a.m., we were done—and we'd finished off the case of beer too.

The next morning at 6 a.m., My uncle and I headed to the office as usual. When we arrived, the company owner met us in the parking lot and told us to get to the housing project and avoid the office for the rest of the day. Confused, we asked what was going on. He explained that we'd laid half of the cork-tone tiles upside down in the mayor's basement. Cork-tone tile has a shiny, smooth side and a porous side, and in the dim light, we hadn't noticed. My uncle had to tear most of it up and replace it at his own expense. I'm sure the poor lighting and long workday played a role, but I'm positive the beer did not have anything to do with it! Needless to say, we never got paid for that custom job!

There was another incident on the same housing project. I was patching the floors when I got careless with the patching material, splashing some on the walls. The project superintendent came in, saw the mess, and demanded that I leave the project and report back to my company for reassignment. I called my uncle and told him what happened. He headed out to the project, and when he arrived, he spread emulsion adhesive (the stuff we used on the floors) all over the walls, about four feet high. Then he called the superintendent over, showed him the mess, and told him never to tell one of his men to leave a project again. The superintendent never bothered me after that.

Another funny incident happened with a different uncle, who was closer to my age and the baby of the family. One day, I was loading cases of tile from our on-site trailer into the van. The trailer was much taller than the van, and while carrying a five-gallon bucket of emulsion, I tripped and fell into the van, hitting my head hard. I knocked myself out. When I came to, I was dazed, but I locked up the trailer, grabbed what I needed, and headed back to the house we were working on. As soon as I got out of the van, my uncle ran over and asked what had happened. I was still fuzzy and asked what he meant. He said, "Son, your face is covered in blood, and you've got a gash in your forehead!" That's when the reality hit me, and I passed out again. They took me to an emergency center to get patched up, and I was told to stay home for a week.

Despite that incident, I got kicked off the project a little while later for something my uncle did! He got into a scuffle with a union business agent, a real jerk. My uncle had cleaned and prepped the floors, and when the BA dropped junk all over the freshly cleaned area, my uncle asked him to wait until we finished. The BA told him to fudge himself and shoved him. My uncle knocked him out cold. The next day, we were both expelled from the project, even though I hadn't even been there!

Now does that seem fair, I was not even there that day, but I got kicked out anyway.

Another memorable episode in my family happened at a large gathering hosted by my uncle, with nearly everyone from my mother's side of the family in attendance. The party took place in my uncle's sloping backyard in a southern suburb of Chicago. My three uncles were there, along with many aunts and cousins. For the first part of the evening, everything went smoothly. People were drinking, laughing, and having a great time.

Then, about halfway through the night, one of my aunts—who had a reputation for being a bit of a drama queen—suddenly lay down on the ground, appearing to have some sort of fit. At least, that's what my mother called it. I was the closest, so I rushed over to see what was wrong. As I knelt beside her, trying to help, my youngest uncle, who was only a few years older than me and the baby of the family, came running over. Without warning, he grabbed me by my shirt, hurled me backward down the slope of the yard, and yelled, "Get away from my sister!" I hit the ground hard and rolled a good distance down the hill.

Seeing red and furious, I jumped up and charged at him. We started fighting until my other uncles stepped in, pulling us apart and warning us there would be no fighting allowed at the party. Tensions flared even more when the uncle I lived with got into a heated argument with his younger brother. They were on the verge of coming to blows when my mother intervened, stopping them from fighting. My uncle turned to me and said, "Let's get out of here. They're not going to let us fight."

We walked around to the front of the house while the uncle I'd been fighting slipped inside and met us in the front yard. Determined to settle things, we decided to drive somewhere more neutral. We got into the car and headed to a dead-end gravel road by some electrical towers, agreeing that only one of us would fight to keep things fair. We flipped a coin, and I won.

We squared off, rolling around in the gravel, punches flying, when suddenly a bunch of police cars came speeding in, sirens blaring. The police chief jumped out, saying they'd received a report that someone was being killed but found us very much alive. I couldn't make sense of it, but whatever floated their boat. To make matters worse, they arrested us for disorderly conduct and threw me and the uncle I was fighting into the back of the same patrol car—and later into the same jail cell, which made even less sense to me.

Meanwhile, the police tried to shove the uncle I lived with into the chief's patrol car. He didn't take kindly to being shoved and almost got into it with the chief. The whole situation turned into a giant mess. Thankfully, our boss from the tile company we all worked for bailed us out so we could make it to work on Monday.

By the next day, we'd all cooled down and apologized to each other. After all, we're family!

CHAPTER 10
LIKE MOTHER, LIKE SON... SORT OF

I had a great mother. I can't say enough about how she treated all of us kids while we were growing up. She was always there for me, even when I got into trouble, which was quite often. When my dad was going crazy disciplining us (that's what he called it, I called it beatings)—especially me and my older sister, since we were the ones who got the worst of it—my mother always stood up for us and tried to stop him. I will always appreciate everything she tried to do for me in my life.

Music was a part of my mom's life too. She could play the guitar, and she used to sing on the radio in Alabama. They called her "The Alabama Sweetheart." She had a good voice, but her timing was a bit off—she couldn't always tell when to come back in after a break in the song. Someone usually had to help her with that. My little sister had the same problem, and my brother, who played the drums, would count in the background to cue her when to come back in. I had my mom's guitar refurbished, and it now hangs on the wall in my basement recording studio. I guess that's where my two brothers, my little sister, and I got our love for music—another thing I have to thank my mom for.

I have so many memories of sitting around with her, playing and singing all those classic country songs she loved. She always came out to see our band when we had a gig close enough for her to attend. I think she even rode on our bus with us a few times (several stories there for another time). Thinking back now, it's crazy to realize, there was an incident in her past where she might not have survived—and we wouldn't be here today.

I once had a conversation with my grandmother (my mom's mom), a tough old southern woman who could handle a shotgun with the same ease she'd handle a broom. She told me a story about my mom when she was a teenager living in the mountains of Alabama. Now, Alabama is known for its mountain lions, including the bobcat, and there are rumors of panthers in those hills—though no one's ever really proved it. According to my grandmother, my mother was walking home through the woods one day (I think it was from school, though I'm not entirely sure) when she heard something behind her. She turned around and came face-to-face with a large, dark-brown panther—or at least that's what she called it. Most likely, it was a big mountain lion.

She said fear took over, and she stood completely still, not knowing what to do. The cat just stared at her. She slowly took a few steps backward, never turning her back on the animal, and each time she stepped back, the cat stepped forward. When my mom later told me her version of the story, she said she knew if she tripped or ran, the cat would have attacked and killed her. So, she kept walking backward all the way through the woods, up onto her front porch, and into the house. The cat followed her right up to the porch, but once she slammed the door and yelled for her parents, it was gone by the time they checked outside.

So, I guess my siblings and I are here today because my mom was good at walking backward through the woods.

That story has always fascinated me, especially because I had my own encounter with a cougar (another name for a mountain lion) while I was cowboying in Idaho. A buddy and I spent time working cattle between the grazing sides of the Grand Tetons in Idaho and Wyoming. It was part of some government arrangement, though I never fully understood the details. We had a camp set up about halfway up the mountain, where we'd sleep after long days of moving cattle. After dinner, I'd usually go for a run. Anyone who knows me knows I've always been a runner—I guess you could say I'm a fitness freak.

On this particular evening, I went for my usual run up the mountain trail, accompanied by a hound dog who had kind of adopted me. He'd race ahead of me, then circle back behind, repeating this pattern over and over. But on this run, something strange happened. The dog ran ahead as usual but then suddenly turned around, barking like crazy, and bolted past me down the trail. He didn't stop by my side—just kept running back toward camp, still barking. Confused, I kept going up the trail.

That's when I saw movement in the trees. I looked up and realized I was staring at a good-sized cougar lounging on a low hanging limb. My heart nearly stopped. I stopped running forward, started running in place, then began jogging backward, just like my mom had done all those years ago. I didn't stick around to see if the cougar moved, and I ran backward all the way down the trail to camp. By the time I got back, the hound was already hiding under one of the trailers—so much for protecting his master.

I guess walking backward or running backwards runs in the family. Thanks, Mom!

I think I understand my mother's fear a little better now. So, like mother, like son... sort of.

CHAPTER 11

SASQUATCH IN CAMP...

During my cowboy days in Idaho and Wyoming, there were several funny incidents that I still laugh about to this day. I already told the story of my encounter with a cougar in the Grand Teton mountains, but that night had more surprises in store. After the scare with the cougar, I shared the story with my fellow cowpunchers, and they all agreed I was lucky not to have been attacked. I felt pretty proud of myself for walking away unscathed.

That evening, we took care of the horses—brushed them down, fed them, and made sure they were ready for the night. Then we headed back to the trailer for a late-night snack of fresh apple pie. We sat around the campfire, telling stories and laughing until our sides hurt. Naturally, some of the stories veered into spooky territory, like the one a cowboy told about seeing a Sasquatch on his last cattle drive.

He said the creature was huge—maybe eight feet tall—and covered in dark fur. Its eyes, glowing red, darted around as it walked through the mountains. The cowboy admitted he felt a wave of fear, worrying the creature might spot him. So, he stayed hidden until it disappeared across the clearing.

That story must've stuck in our heads more than we realized because later that night, we all went to bed with a bit of unease. After my shower, I hit the sack in my part of the trailer. There were two of us assigned to each trailer, with one bedroom at each end.

I'm not sure how long I'd been asleep, but suddenly, the trailer started shaking like we were in the middle of an earthquake.

I jumped out of bed and rushed into the front room, just as my buddy came running from his side of the trailer. "What the hell is going on?" he yelled. "It feels like something's shaking the trailer!"

"Yeah, no kidding!" I shouted back. "What do you think it is?"

Then he gave me a look and said, "Why don't you go out and see?"

I could tell we were both thinking the same thing—that an eight-foot-tall Sasquatch was outside, rocking our trailer like a tin can. I looked him dead in the eye and said, "Hell no! You go out and see!"

We kept arguing for a minute, neither of us wanting to be the one to face the supposed Sasquatch, until finally, we agreed to go outside together and check it out.

As it turned out, we had forgotten to lock the corral gate properly when we put the horses up that night, and the animals had wandered out. One of the horses had an itchy back and was using the side of our trailer to scratch itself, causing the whole thing to shake like crazy. We were relieved it wasn't a hungry Sasquatch after all but dealing with the horses being loose cost us most of the next day. We spent hours chasing them down before we could even start our work. Needless to say, we got plenty of grief from the other cowboys for leaving the corral gate open.

Another memorable incident from one of the cattle drives involved a buddy of mine chasing down a stray. When you're moving cattle, there are always some that like to stray away from the main herd. That's why we had cattle dogs, but it was also our job to round up any cattle that wandered off.

On this particular day, it seemed like the cattle had decided to make our lives miserable. Small groups kept breaking off and heading in different directions. One group of five headed straight for the Snake River and swam across to a small island in the middle. The owner motioned for me to follow him across the river to round them up. That was my first time crossing a river on horseback, and I wasn't sure what to expect. When we got into the water, I felt myself float up a little, clinging to my horse as we crossed. Once we reached the other side, my horse sank down into a muddy patch but managed to get back up without throwing me off. We herded the cattle back across the river and rejoined the main group.

Just as we got back, two more cows took off down a mountain trail. I was about to head after them when my buddy yelled, "I'll get them!" and galloped off.

I watched him ride after the cattle, and everything seemed fine until he approached a large tree that had fallen across the trail. At first, it looked like he was going to jump it, but then his horse hit the brakes hard, stopping right in front of the tree. My buddy, however, didn't stop. He sailed right over the horse's head and landed with a solid thump on the other side of the tree trunk.

A few minutes later, he limped back to the herd, pulling his horse along by the reins. He'd hurt his back and leg in the fall, but that didn't stop the rest of us from laughing at his predicament. It's hard not to laugh when you picture it in your mind—my buddy flying through the air like some kind of rodeo clown.

There were definitely some fun times up in the Tetons—just ask my buddy.

CHAPTER 12
NO MOONSHINE INVOLVED THIS TIME...

I've already told you about my moonshine adventures and the chaos that followed in high school, where kids were getting loaded on moonshine mixed with Pepsi or Coke (whichever they preferred). Looking back, it seems I've been something of a rebel most of my life. Mischief, mayhem, or trouble always seemed to follow me, and this story is no exception.

Before we dive into this one, let me give you a little more insight into my "bad boy" reputation during those high school years. Skipping classes was no big deal to me—sometimes I'd even skip whole days. But despite that, most of my teachers liked me. They were always willing to help me keep my grades up, and I owe them a lot for shaping me into a better student and, eventually, a better person. I'm certain their patience is what helped me finally get my act together.

Back then, I was an A-student—well, technically, an "E" student, since the top grade used to stand for "Excellent." My report cards were always full of E+ marks... until high school, when I discovered girls, partying, and everything else that came with it. To be fair, I didn't exactly start off on the wrong foot by myself. I blame my sister—well, sort of.

On the first day of school, my homeroom teacher went down the list of names and paused when she got to mine. She asked if I was my sister's brother and then said, "If you're anything like her, your trouble." She made me move to the front row, right under her nose, to keep an eye on me. That moment pretty much set the tone for the rest of my high school days.

Now, I don't blame her—my sister was notorious. I won't go into all the details but suffice it to say she was kicked out of not one, but three schools. The Last school required a signature by my mother when she got on the bus and a signature of the bus driver when she got to school. Now I ask you, how can someone get kicked out of a closely monitored school system like that? Let me further make my case about my sister's fiery nature and possibly my ability to do dumb things.

One afternoon, my sister and I were home alone. She was busy washing dishes, one of her regular chores, while I sat at the kitchen table, bored out of my mind. On the table was this small, round aluminum cup, and I started fiddling with it to pass the time. I'd tip it onto its side and then flick the edge so it would spin, making a loud clattering sound as it rattled against the Formica tabletop before somehow landing back upright. It amused me, so I kept at it, relishing the racket.

After a few spins, my sister looked over her shoulder and sighed, "Can you stop that? It's getting on my nerves." I said "Okay" but couldn't resist giving it one more flick. Then another. Each time, she'd stop and ask me to quit, and each time, I'd give her a nod of agreement before flicking it again. Finally, she snapped, "I'm not going to ask you again!"

Naturally, I ignored her and slapped the cup again, watching it spin to my amusement. That must have been the final straw because, the next thing I knew, I felt a heavy blow to the back of my head that nearly knocked me senseless. Many people might say that explains some of the dumb things I did throughout my life!

When my vision finally cleared, I realized what had happened: my sister, mid-dishwashing, had grabbed the cast-iron skillet and whacked me on the head. She'd hit me so hard she broke the skillet clean in half. She stood there, a little scared she might have actually hurt me. But as soon as I came to my senses, I got to my feet and punched her in the stomach, sending her backward onto the couch in the living room. She sat there, clutching her stomach and glaring at me.

We were both silent for a moment, each of us nursing our bruises, but I could tell the gears were turning in her head. Suddenly, she leapt up, grabbed another black iron skillet from the stove, and started after me. I took one look at her determined face, and I was out the back door, tearing down the gangway. She chased me, skillet in hand, until finally, she threw it at me. It sailed past, missing me but smashing against the concrete, breaking the second skillet. She stormed off, declaring that she wasn't coming back until Mom got rid of "the monster that lived there"—namely, me.

Another time, the two of us were tasked with painting the iron railings at the front of the house. My sister was bent over, working on the lower part of the railing, and, well, I just couldn't resist. I reached over and gave her a good smack on the butt. I knew she'd come up swinging, so I immediately ducked and tried to turn away. I was shirtless—it was a hot day—and she didn't hesitate. She spun around, clawed at me with her long nails, and dragged them down my back, leaving deep scratch marks. I was left with rows of cuts and bits of skin and blood under her nails.

Let's just say, I got the worst end of that deal. I couldn't wear a shirt for over two weeks because of the gashes across my back.

So I rest my case! She ended up in Alabama with relatives, where she finally got her life on track. I guess that's why I spent a lot of time in Alabama, too. Seems like getting kicked out of places runs in the family.

But let me get to the main event—this particular Friday night. The school hosted what they called "Activity Night," where students could relax, play basketball or volleyball, listen to music, and dance. I shouldn't have been there, honestly. I'd cut school the entire day, which was a huge no-no. But I still showed up, thinking it would go unnoticed. Spoiler alert: It didn't.

My best friend and I had plans to meet up with two girls from our class. I really liked one of them, and my buddy liked her sister, so we were hoping for a double date. While waiting for the girls, we got pulled into a basketball game with some guys, including a group from a rival high school across town. During the game, one of them made a nasty comment about the girl I liked.

Now, I've never been one to back down from an insult, especially when it involved a girl I was sweet on. So, I told him exactly what I thought of his remark. Predictably, he fired back with more trash talk, trying to show off in front of his friends. Things escalated fast. They had to pull us apart, and the teacher in charge warned us: no fighting on his watch.

But I wasn't about to let it go. I told the guy we'd settle this outside, since he had to leave the activity night sometime, and me and my buddy went to wait. Standing out there, it hit me—there were eight of them and only two of us. That was a problem. So, I ran up the street to where our crew hung out and rounded up a few of my buddies. Now, these guys were what the news called "hoodlums" back then—leather jackets, long hair, bad attitudes, the works. They were always up for a fight, and that night, I was ready to give them one.

Looking back, I really should've thought it through a bit more.

When Activity Night ended, we were all standing around outside, acting tough, waiting for the guys to come out. Now, this was a different time—back then, we settled things with our fists, not guns. It didn't take long for someone to say the wrong thing, and the pushing and shoving started. Within minutes, a full-out brawl had erupted. It was chaos—kids fighting all over the place, fists flying, teachers yelling, and the school cop, who had no hope of controlling any of it, calling for backup. Squad cars showed up, but by then, the fight had taken over the whole street.

Amid all the punches and shouting, I somehow never found the guy I was looking for—the one who insulted my girl. I never got the satisfaction of punching him out.

The next day, the whole thing was on the news. They called it a riot, caused by "unruly students." Some kids even spent the night in jail, waiting for their parents to come bail them out. All of that was because I wanted to fight one guy over one stupid comment.

And in the end, I didn't even get the guy I wanted to punch out. Go figure.

CHAPTER 13
WHERE'S THE CHICKEN WIRE?

I love music—just about any genre, really. From original country to jazz, '70s rock, and the golden oldies of the '50s and '60s, it's all a part of me. I'm sure I got that from my mother because my dad never seemed interested in music at all. My brothers and sisters share my passion as well. Growing up, I was heavily influenced by the sounds of Merle Haggard, David Allan Coe, The Rolling Stones, The Beatles, Charlie Daniels, Lynyrd Skynyrd, and The Marshall Tucker Band.

My brother and I eventually formed a Southern Country Rock band. For over six years, we played across the Midwest and southern states. My brother was the drummer—now, for those of you who don't know, a drummer is the guy who hangs out with real musicians (he'll appreciate that joke). I was one of two lead singers and shared lead guitar duties, while also playing rhythm guitar on a flat-top acoustic for certain songs. And because everyone loves a beautiful girl in a band, my younger sister joined us as a lead singer—she'll like that line!

We played just about every venue you could think of auditoriums, bars, fairs, festivals, even semi-truck trailers and private stages set up in people's backyards. We had a pretty strong following, and we even got to open for some major national acts a few times. Those shows were always a blast and usually involved plenty of drinking.

In 1988, my life took a turn when I severed my left arm between the wrist and elbow in an accident. I didn't know a person could hurt that much and still live. I was certain I was going to die. But thanks to the quick thinking of a retired paramedic and a fast-responding ambulance, I survived. It took eight years of surgeries, physical therapy, and a lot of hard work before I was able to play music again.

Nowadays, I still get together with band members and new members and we play special events around the Midwest. There are a lot of stories from our time on the road, but one gig stands out.

We were hired to play a large bar in a northern Chicago suburb. Everything started off smoothly. We loaded up our bus— not a fancy tour bus, but a renovated school bus we used to haul ourselves and all our gear. Honestly, we sometimes felt like the *Beverly Hillbillies*. The bar was more like a resort, with a bunch of cabins for rent along a river. It had a good-sized stage, and we were able to park the bus right next to a side door that opened directly to the stage.

Unloading and setting up the equipment is the worst part of any gig, and every musician knows it. We mic'ed up the drums, checked the guitars and bass (another guy who hangs around real musicians), and did a sound check for all the vocals. After a couple of songs to tweak the settings, we were ready to go. So far, so good.

Our first set went well. The place was about half full, and the crowd gave us some good applause. We took a few song requests, as long as we had a clue on how to play them and had a few drinks ourselves. The second set was just as smooth. Everything seemed to be going great.

49

Then came the third set. Right in the middle of a song, we heard a loud roar coming from the parking lot. It turns out this bar was a popular spot for a local biker gang. The door swung open, and in came a large group of bikers. Now, I've got nothing against bikers—hell, I rode a Harley myself for years with a group of great guys I'm proud to call brothers—but this crowd had a different vibe.

We kept playing, but then my bandmate, who was like a little brother to me, decided to sing a song with the following lyrics:

And it's up against the wall, Redneck Mother
Mother, who has raised her son so well
He's thirty-four and drinking in a honky tonk
Just kicking hippie's asses and raising hell.

Only, he changed that last line to:

"Kicking biker's asses and raising hell."

Good job, Little Brother!

That didn't go over too well with the bikers. There were some comments thrown around, and trust me, they weren't nice. Now, I am not sure if my little brother's change of song lyrics cause this to happen but it sure did not help. Then, out of nowhere, a scrawny biker got into it with a big-built woman over what was being said. She grabbed him by the neck like someone choking a chicken and punched him like a grown man. He flew over a table and crashed into a couple of other bikers who were sitting there. Naturally, they jumped up, and before we knew it, the whole bar was in an all-out brawl.

We kept playing, believe it or not, while chairs and tables were being flipped over. People were rushing for the door, and bottles started flying through the air. The bar owner was yelling at us to keep playing, hoping it would somehow calm everyone down and get them back to drinking and dancing. Meanwhile, we were dodging bottles and kicking away guys who were fighting too close to the stage.

The whole thing happened fast, but it felt like it would never end. Finally, my brother—who was the acknowledged leader of the band—yelled, "Let's get our stuff and get out of here!"

We stopped playing, grabbed our instruments, and quickly loaded everything back into the bus. Thankfully, we had parked it right by the stage door. While we loaded up, we had to dodge the brawling crowd, but we managed to get out of there without getting hurt or losing any gear.

As we sped away, I suggested that next time, we invest in some chicken wire to hang in front of the stage—just in case.

Oh, and I am pretty sure we never did get paid for that gig!

On the way home, we stopped at a toll booth. My little brother—yep, the same guy who sang about the bikers, pulled another stunt. Instead of handing the toll booth attendant money, he handed her a southern fried chicken leg that my mom had packed for us. She just grinned, shook her head, thanked us for the chicken and waved us through. Nothing like southern fried chicken! Just ask Colonel Sanders.

CHAPTER 14
GHOST IN THE HOUSE

One of the most unusual occurrences in my life was meeting a ghost—yes, you read that right, a ghost. Though we weren't formally introduced, we stared at each other for what felt like an eternity one night. Let me explain what happened.

At one point, my brother and I were managing one of the most well-known country nightclubs in the Midwest. This club boasted what was likely the longest bar in the city—over 100 feet long. We spent countless nights dealing with the ups and downs of running a nightclub, interacting with a mix of customers, bands, and their members. Running a bar where live bands played every Friday and Saturday night was no small task. We were open until 4 a.m., so every weekend turned into a marathon.

The nature of the business brought plenty of challenges. Many nights, we dealt with patrons who'd had too much to drink or couples arguing over someone paying too much attention to the guys in the band. Sometimes, the arguments were over an insult or jealousy, and other times, someone was trying to win over a date who clearly wasn't interested. We often found ourselves stepping in to break up fights—sometimes between guys, and sometimes even between women. Weekends were far from boring, but the drama didn't stop there. During the week, we had to handle similar situations, proving it wasn't just the weekend crowd that caused trouble. I guess it's just how people are when they're drinking.

At times, I acted as the bouncer; other times, my brother or one of our employees would step in. Being a bouncer in a nightclub is a unique mix of authority, conflict management, and quick decision-making. The atmosphere, with its ever-changing mix of people and loud music, keeps you on high alert. De-escalating fights, monitoring potential troublemakers, and keeping the crowd under control—these were all part of the job. It was definitely not as easy as it looked. One example I remember was one night, a young guy suddenly jumped up and started punching and slapping the woman he was with. My brother and another bouncer immediately stepped in, stopped him, and began escorting him to the door, insisting he had to leave. While they were doing this, the very woman who had just been used as a punching bag started hitting my brother in the back, screaming at him to let the guy go and that it was none of his business if they had a fight. Go figure. There more than a few tense moments during that time which is another story for another time.

One part of the job was dealing with patrons who wanted to have a drink with us. Some people, you just couldn't say no to, and by the end of the night, I usually had a few drinks before heading home. After one particularly long night, my brother and I stopped for breakfast before making our way home. At the time, I was living with him and his family. Exhausted, I went straight to my bedroom, which was at the end of a long hallway. Several bedrooms lined the hall, with the living room off to the side, and the kitchen at the opposite end.

I remember taking a quick shower before collapsing into bed. I must have fallen asleep immediately, but I woke up suddenly, feeling disoriented. My body was freezing, and I was trembling uncontrollably. Then, my bedroom door creaked open.

Standing at the foot of my bed was a young woman dressed in what looked like an old-fashioned gown. I was confused and tried to get up, but I couldn't move. My body was completely paralyzed—except for my eyes. We locked eyes for what felt like forever. I don't know how long we stared at each other, but then, as silently as she'd appeared, she turned and walked out of the room and down the hallway.

The second she left, I could move again. I jumped out of bed and ran to the door. There she was, calmly walking down the hallway toward the kitchen. I followed her, but when I reached the kitchen, it was completely empty. That's when the shivers really set in.

The next morning, I told my brother and nephew about what had happened, half-expecting them to laugh it off. Instead, they looked at each other knowingly. They told me they'd seen the same young woman more than once while watching TV in the living room. She would walk past the door, head down the hall, and turn into the kitchen. But whenever they went to check, the kitchen was always empty.

Curious and a little freaked out, we did some digging and spoke to the owner of the building. What he told us sent chills down my spine. About ten years earlier, a young woman had been killed in the very bedroom I was staying in. According to him, her body had been dragged down the hall to the kitchen, and the person responsible was never caught. We weren't the first to see her walking from the bedroom to the kitchen. Apparently, previous tenants had similar encounters.

That was all I needed to hear. I didn't spend another night in that bedroom. We moved out shortly after that, and as far as I was concerned, I was gone for good. Some things you just don't mess with—ghosts being one of them.

That wasn't the only time I experienced something strange, something that left me paralyzed, unable to move any part of my body except my eyes. To this day, it remains a mystery. Let me explain.

My dad had bought a new house in a suburb just west of Chicago. Since it was a new build, he was allowed to handle certain parts of the work himself, like laying the floor tile, installing the wall tile in the bathrooms, and painting. It saved him a lot on the cost of the house. Since I worked with my uncles in the tile business, most of the work fell to me—especially all the floor and wall tile installation.

After finishing up my regular day working on a housing project, I'd head over to my dad's place and continue working there into the night. By then, I was usually exhausted from a full day of laying tile, and after working on my dad's house, I'd be even more worn out. Some nights, I'd crash on an old couch in the basement—the only piece of furniture in the house at the time.

One night, I was sleeping on that couch when I suddenly woke up. I'm not sure what caused me to wake, but when I opened my eyes, I was staring at what looked like a glowing white ball of light, with rays of light shooting out from it. The room was completely silent, and when I tried to sit up, I realized I couldn't move. My body was paralyzed. All I could do was stare at this strange light, a feeling of fear creeping in as the minutes dragged on. It felt like an eternity. Then, just as mysteriously as it appeared, the glowing light began to fade. As soon as it disappeared, I found I could move again.

I didn't waste any time—I got up and left the house, and I didn't spend another night there while I finished the work.

To this day, I don't know what that was. It was different from the time a ghost—or whatever you want to call it—showed up in my bedroom.

I just hope I never experience anything like that again.

CHAPTER 15
THE BAD BOYS OF...

When tragedy struck and I lost part of my left arm between the elbow and wrist, I thought my days of making music with my brother and nephew were over. I didn't think I would survive, but the prayers and unwavering support from my family, friends, and fellow musicians pulled me through. Eventually, I found the strength to play again.

My recovery lasted over several grueling years, involving a second surgery and countless hours of difficult therapy. During that time, more than 30 different devices were fitted to my arm, some with wires threaded through my fingernails, making me look like a nightmarish version of Freddy Krueger. It was a slow and painful process.

Once I was strong enough, my routine settled into a rhythm: driving to the hospital for therapy and then heading to work. This pattern lasted for years. Occasionally, I would pick up hitchhikers near the hospital, not realizing the implications until a particularly eerie encounter. One day, I offered a ride to a young man who seemed friendly enough. Unbeknownst to me, the hospital's far end housed a mental health ward—a fact I learned the hard way.

The young man explained why he stood away from that side of the hospital, saying, "People never stop for you there. Go figure!" As we talked, his questions took a dark turn: "Have you ever thought about dying?" and "When I die, I always figured I'd take someone with me, so I wouldn't go alone. How do you feel about suicide?" Seems like a decent way to go, he said. His words made my skin crawl. I lied, claiming I had to turn off soon, even though it wasn't true. He tried to insist on staying, but I wasn't about to let that happen.

I pulled into a gas station, pretending to answer an urgent phone call. I told him the doctor needed me back at the hospital. Thankfully, he decided not to come along and stayed at the gas station, chatting with the attendant, I never picked up another hitchhiker again.

Throughout my recovery, I visited my brother's band performances and occasionally joined them to sing. One night, a fellow band leader was impressed by my singing and asked me to be a lead vocalist in his band. I accepted and began rehearsing regularly.

Our new band had two lead singers, and we developed a unique sound. Initially, the bass player was skeptical, later admitting, "Who's this cocky dude acting like he knows everything?" But over time, he became like a brother to me and my best friend. He was the kind of guy who kept everyone laughing, even maintaining a journal of our gigs. One memorable entry referred to me, saying, "Tony danced with a thousand girls tonight."

During that performance, the other singer had me set down my guitar and step off the stage and requested all the ladies in the bar to come up and dance with me. I danced with nearly every woman in the bar that night. It was a night filled with laughter and unforgettable memories. His journal is worthy of an entire chapter of stories.

For over five years, I sang and played guitar with the band, experiencing incredible camaraderie and unforgettable opportunities. We played at clubs, fairs, and even opened for national acts. The bond we shared made every moment worthwhile. It took years of surgeries and relentless therapy to play the guitar again, but when I finally did, it felt amazing to be back on stage with my guitar in my hand.

One of the funniest episodes from that time revolved around our "Bad Boys of Country" stickers. We developed a reputation as a bad boy, hard-drinking band that played red-hot music and entertained the crowd. Fans began regularly sending rounds of tequila to the stage, and we happily accepted. People started calling us the bad boys of country. My best friend, the bass player, made stickers that read "Bad Boys of Country," which our fans enthusiastically plastered around the venues.

At one gig, a group of women—our "bad girls of country"—covered the bar and bathrooms with stickers. The bar owner was furious, and we had to return the next day to scrape them off. It was far less amusing then, but the legend of the Bad Boys of Country lives on in stories told across the Midwest.

Another unforgettable night involved a persistent fan. A group sat in front of the stage, and the leader approached us, offering $20 to play "Achy Breaky Heart" for his girlfriend. Naturally, for $20, we would attempt to play anything. So we played it and his girlfriend loved it. He then came back repeatedly, offering another $20 each time we played it, earning a surprising amount of money in the process. Another great night for the bad boys.

Then there was the drummer's birthday, a night none of us will ever forget. Bands are known for drinking, and we were no exception. While most of the guys drank beer, I preferred tequila.

That night, the tequila flowed freely, and the bar patrons kept sending us shots. As we played our third set, at one point, fans sent 20 shots for each of us in one 45-minute set. That is probably the catalyst that put us over the intoxication limit. By then, we were thoroughly wasted.

During a Southern rock number, "Gimme Three Steps," the birthday boy drummer stood up mid-song and announced he was leaving. I tried to tell him; you can't leave we are still on stage playing. When I tried to get him back on the drums, he said. "See how big I am and how small you are?", I am leaving, he retorted. He was a big boy for sure. Thankfully, I got him to finish the set. It was another wild night with the bad boys.

One gig stands out for its near brawl. The other lead singer was somewhat of ladies' man (I am sure he will like that comment). The ladies always seem to search him out and want to buy him drinks, dance with him and in some cases date him. I have to say he did nothing to dissuade them from this kind of activity.... imagine that. One might say he really seemed to enjoy it. At this particular gig, he was being his normal bad boy, girl chasing self and if my memory serves me correct, he was paying too much attention to one pretty young lady. Apparently, her boyfriend or wanna-be boyfriend did not appreciate it. The bass player, and I saw this big unhappy guy heading toward our fellow musician, with intensions of starting a fight with our friend. We always had each other's back. So, we moved to intercept him, backed him into a corner and explained to him the current facts of life, basically, what would happen to him if he continued with his plan to jump our friend. He determined his best course of action was to forget it and leave, which he did. Hopefully our friend appreciates the two of us keeping this big guy off of him that night. Just another great night for the bad boys of country.

I'd be remiss not to give a shout-out to the two strong women who kept us grounded: my wife and the bass player's wife. They are the real reason we got our lives back on track, from wild bad boys to respectable family men.....well almost respectable!

Made in the USA
Monee, IL
30 November 2024

71802620R00039